THE
NEW RADNOR
BRANCH

The
NEW RADNOR
BRANCH

NICHOLAS de COURTAIS

FOREWORD

To describe the railways in the area of Kington such that the line between New Radnor and Kington receives a volume to itself might seem to be disproportionately generous. But the fruits of research are unpredictable, and I have been blessed with sufficient material that an overall narrative of the area would have been unbalanced by its inclusion; the availability of photographs covering almost the entire length of the New Radnor line, due no doubt to its relative accessibility, has enabled the route to be described in a depth not possible for the rest of the lines associated with Kington.

Furthermore, the line has such a particular evocation for both myself and my publisher that we felt perfectly justified in devoting a separate volume to it; by doing this, the work has unwittingly taken on quite a different character to that originally envisaged – more of an intimate portrait. This is in no small measure due to the inclusion of the memorable photography of the late Richard Jobson, New Radnor's doctor from 1937 until his sad death in 1977. The photographs date from the 1940s, and evoke the period with an unmistakable style; his use of filters and a separate light meter (he possessed a Watkins) no doubt add to this.

This volume therefore stands on its own as a presentation of the history and life of this short railway line. A further volume will, in due course, complete the narrative of this network of lines, and deal more fully with the early history of them, and I hope that readers will wish to acquire both books. With another volume in the offing, I also hope readers will take me to task over any errors, and of course additional material will be gladly received, whether on New Radnor or the remainder of the Kington network of lines.

Nicholas de Courtais

Near New Radnor.   *R. H. Jobson*

INTRODUCTION

THE borderland between England and Wales is an area of great natural beauty. Within the sparsely-populated central region lies the former county of Radnorshire, with miles of moorland ridges stretching to the horizon, dominated by the dark mass of Radnor Forest. A brief perusal of a map of the area will reveal the existence of a small village called Old Radnor, situated about halfway between Kington and New Radnor. There is a tradition that this was once a thriving town, confirmed to some extent by the occasional discovery of old building foundations in the vicinity – it was apparently destroyed during civil dissentation in the year 990. The Mercians subsequently took possession of the place (then called Maesfed Hen), and Earl Harold established his seat nearby, at a place he named Radrenove (New Radnor); the descriptions of 'Old' and 'New' Radnor are therefore now one thousand years old. The County of Radnorshire has now lost its identity, but when it was created in 1536, New Radnor became the shire town. This function was transferred to Presteign after the Civil War, along with the local assizes.

The railway history of the area began with the building of the Kington Railway [sic] of 1818. This was constructed as a narrow gauge, horse-powered tramway, running between Eardisley and the limestone quarries near Old Radnor. The function of the tramway was to transport coal to the kilns at Dolyhir, and to despatch the lime produced, along with stone of various grades.

This early view of Kington shows the exit taken by trains for New Radnor and the first of the river bridges. The tall signal post in the foreground is for the up home signal, which at this time was on the station side of the road overbridge. This placed the engine shed siding outside the home signal and in the section to New Radnor. The home signal was later relocated, on a much shorter post, further away from the station, beyond the engine siding points (see page 30). *Collection Rev. D. A. Tipper*

Further developments took place during 1856/7 with the construction of the Leominster & Kington Railway, a standard gauge line linking the two towns. This $13\frac{1}{2}$ mile-long branch between Kington Junction and Kington opened on 20th August 1857 and was worked initially by the contractor, Brassey. From June 1862, the line was leased and worked by the West Midland Railway.

The railway map of the area was effectively completed during the 1870s with the arrival of the Kington & Eardisley Company. This concern reached Kington only by virtue of running powers over the L & KR line from its junction with the latter at Titley. A similar arrangement existed at the southern end of the line, with the K & E exercising running rights into the Midland Railway's Eardisley station. The branch was opened on 3rd August 1874. Small companies have often been vulnerable to takeover by larger concerns, and the Kington & Eardisley narrowly escaped such a fate, having aroused the interest of the Midland; the railway history of the area might be very different had this attempt been successful.

In 1873, the Kington & Eardisley had obtained authorisation to build an extension from Kington to New Radnor as a preliminary stage of a scheme to construct a line westwards to Rhayader; this $6\frac{1}{2}$ mile section was opened on 25th September 1875 (shortly after the inauguration of the Leominster & Kington's Presteign branch). However, the grander scheme failed to materialize due to lack of financial support and New Radnor, laid out as a through station, became a sleepy terminus. Its facilities, minimal as they were, soon appeared to be rather excessive in view of the level of traffic generated.

And so began the life of what, in due course, became just another GWR branch line. As was so often the case, the railway started its existence as a locally-based, legally-distinct company with local sponsorship and board of directors, but under an agreement worked by the GWR.

During its 75 or so years, the New Radnor 'extension' led a relatively quiet life, perhaps barely justifying its existence. Despite this, the line had an undeniable appeal, travelling as it did through an area of outstanding natural beauty.

Doug Gunney, Leominster fireman, is grinning at Dick Jobson in this unusual view of the Radnor Goods, almost certainly through Lyonshall Park on the eastern approach to Kington and quite likely during the appalling winter of 1947.   *R. H. Jobson*

CHAPTER ONE

BUILDING THE LINE

THE Kington Tramway was still very much alive in 1873, as evidenced by the statement of accounts for the half-year ending 31st December: 'plates for repair of tramway ... £25 2s 6d'. However, the increasing remoteness of the lands beyond the quarries made the contemplation of any further railway building somewhat incomprehensible, especially in retrospect.

The decision to promote the New Radnor extension had been taken at a board meeting of the Kington & Eardisley Company in October 1872. This resolution arose out of the 'expediency of going to Parliament for further powers at Eardisley when the same Bill could authorise the conversion of the tramway to Old Radnor and then extend the line to New Radnor'. The idea of building a line to Aberystwyth had been voiced as far back as about 1850, although the time had hardly been ripe! New Radnor, though smaller than many a village, was considered to be a justifiable interim goal for the scheme, as it was a larger community than anywhere else on the 'extension' (as it was henceforth to be known). It was believed that there would be a demand for both passenger and goods services in addition to traffic from the lime

works at Old Radnor. At a board meeting of the company on 14th December 1872, a proof of the proposed new Bill was considered, and Danzey Green Price (his father, Sir Richard, was vice chairman, briefly MP for Radnorshire, and deeply involved with the Central Wales Railway) was requested to negotiate for the provision of the Parliamentary deposit on the best terms within his powers.

By April 1873 the K & ER's retained engineer, G. Wells Owen, had been paid £100 and instructed to 'get out working plans'. By June, when the share and debenture holders had authorised the new capital to be raised (the Act having obtained the Royal Assent on 16th of that month), he had been further instructed to prepare a contract.

Meanwhile, the contractor Charles Chambers, no less than the third to be taken on by the company, was successfully fulfilling his task of completing the line northwards into Titley. When building a railway through Kirkby Stephen, he is on record as riding on horseback through the navvies' camp wielding a whip in order to get the men out on site. There was no doubt about letting Chambers have the contract for the building of the

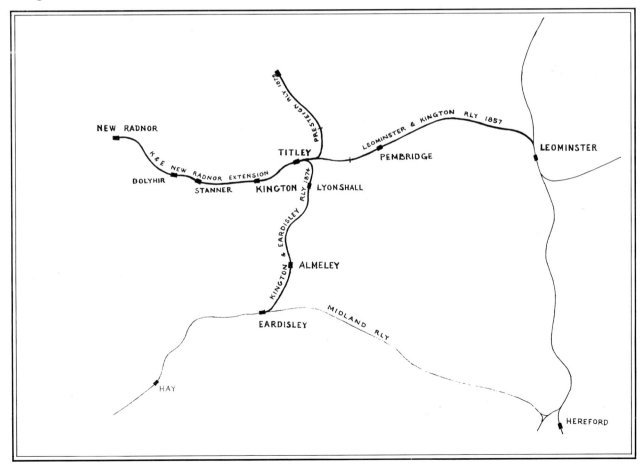

3

K & E.RY (EXTN. TO NEW RADNOR)

STATION BUILDING AT THE LIMEKILNS

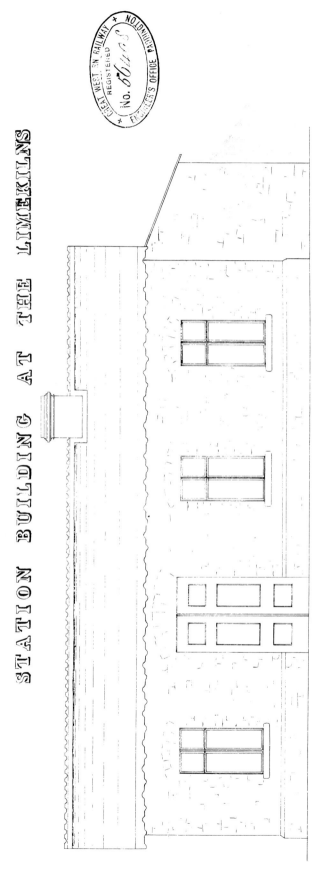

ELEVATION

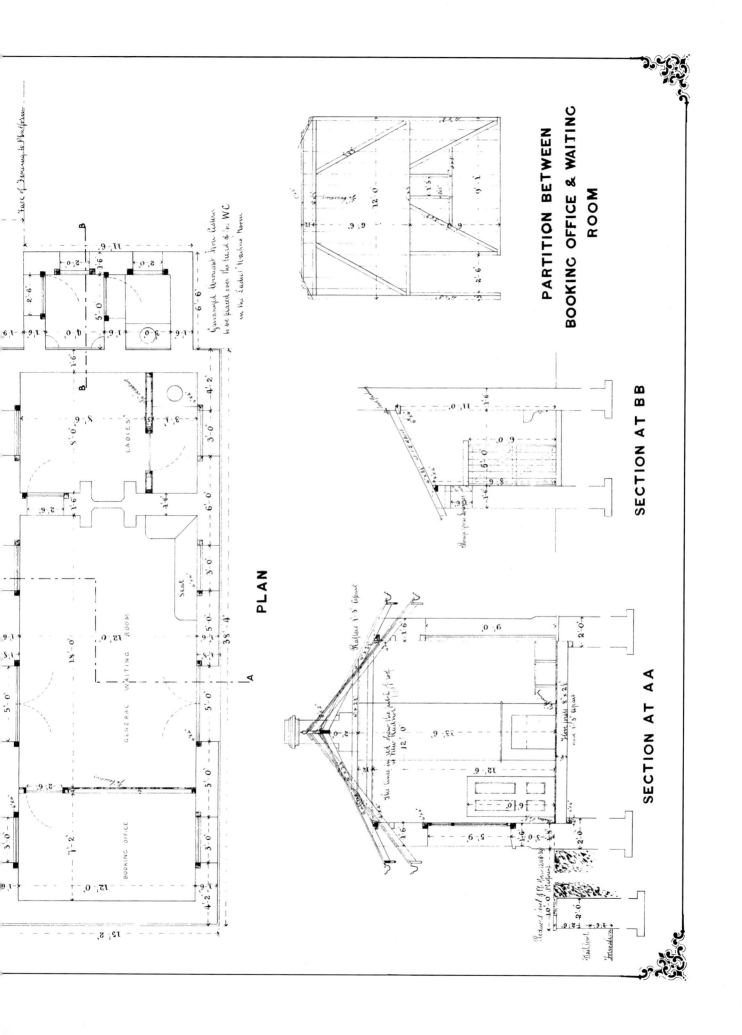

PLAN

PARTITION BETWEEN
BOOKING OFFICE & WAITING
ROOM

SECTION AT BB

SECTION AT AA

extension – the K & E had already had its fingers burnt too often! The contract was signed on 26th July 1873, and provided for a constructional cost of £44,000.

The Act itself authorised the company to make a railway 6 miles 3 furlongs 18 chains in length, commencing 'by a junction with the Leominster and Kington Railway at Kington, in the parish of Kington, in the County of Hereford, and terminating in the parish of New Radnor, in the county of Radnor'. The railway was to finish 'in a field the property of the Reverend Sir Gilbert Frankland Lewis Bt. (a director of the K & E) in the occupation of James Nibblett, John Jones and others at the fence dividing the aforesaid field from the lane leading from New Radnor to the Bryn, usually known as the Smatcher Lane at a point seventy two yards or thereabouts from the junction of the said lane with the turnpike road leading from New Radnor to Kington'.

The deposited plans show the new line leaving Kington on an alignment between the goods shed and passenger station, with a level crossing over the road to Titley. In the event, two new platforms with a new station building were erected to the north of the L & K terminus, which was retained as a goods yard. The new station building and waiting shelter were designed by G. Wells Owen, and were accordingly architecturally consistent with the proposed designs for the rest of the extension. The Kington to Presteign road was realigned, and crossed the railway by a new bridge, known as 'Sunset bridge'. The close proximity of the Langdale Brook, despite its diversion, added to a congested arrangement and the new Kington station was, of all the 'lost' termini, surely the most inelegant; it was also destined to be subject to flooding The old L & K station became totally incorporated into the goods yard of the revised arrangements, and although the station master's residence remained unchanged, the station offices eventually became a feed store. The new passenger station was conventional enough with up and down platforms, but no footbridge was provided; whether this saving was a harbinger of infrequent traffic, or due to the fact that up trains often left from the down platform remains a point for speculation. This latter practice was to be the cause of at least one accident. It is thought that the provision of water cranes dated from the opening of this new station. They were supplied from a tank at the end of the up platform. The provision of an engine shed here was in lieu of one at New Radnor – which might have been expected by the unwary – but then that station was only a temporary terminus, wasn't it?

The initial goal (but not the *raison d'être*) of the extension was the quarries, and as the GWR had only agreed to two stations, drawings were prepared only for these.

The Act, as we have already seen, received Royal Assent on 16th June 1873, and the Engineer lost no time. On 19th August, he reported that 'The Chief portion of this Line has been staked out on the ground and the land plans prepared. The working Drawings of the Bridges and

other works near Kington, and Floodgates are nearly ready and the Contractor is prepared to commence work as soon as he is put in possession of any of the land.' There were, however, difficulties in negotiating the purchase price of some of the land, Wells Owen writing to one landowner:

'The amount you require for 4 acres was discussed at our Board meeting. In order to avoid severance the Company have agreed to take land which they do not require and pay the additional heavy sum. We think you have not sufficiently taken into consideration the Company is struggling to make the line somewhat under difficulties and cannot give extreme prices for the land'

and to another:

'You cannot expect the Company to pay for the bed of the River or Stream ... at a price per acre as if it were land or as if you could convey it to us in any way but as a stream course.'

But negotiating sales to public bodies is an old sport, and much the same tactics would be used today; the Board of Trade valuer was, however, able to save the company some £500 in compensation.

The line was easy to construct, being relatively level for much of its length. The Act provided for four level crossings, one of which (in Kington) was to be supplemented by a foot-bridge. Station buildings were to be in a style comparable to those already in hand on the Titley to Eardisley line. The structure at the lime kilns, later to be called Dolyhir, was a simple affair (rather similar to Almeley, but longer) whilst that at New Radnor was to be a larger version of Lyonshall, with half-hipped gable ends, finials, patterned roof tiles and a short bay projecting onto the platform with its own matching half-hipped gable.

In July 1874, two days after the Eardisley to Titley line had been sanctioned by the BOT, the board discussed 'the question' of Stanner station. It was resolved that the Engineer be requested to furnish a plan at the smallest practicable cost. Surprisingly, in spite of the company's financial situation, they also resolved to undertake a share of the deposit of £5,000 for the Worcester to Aberystwyth Bill; the GW declined to pay their share(!), and there the matter of any further railway building beyond Radnor effectively died for all time. However, the Bill for the line as far as Rhayader was passed, and plans were prepared for construction work up to Penybont. The resolution to build Stanner station was passed on 3rd October, using the drawing of the station at the lime kilns. A proposed station at Harpton for the Reverend Gilbert Lewis (who lived at Harpton Court), was vetoed by the Great Western.

The directors report for August reveals that Chambers had taken full advantage of a fine summer, and the works had been 'vigorously' proceeded with. Most of the earthworks had been completed, and he had commenced laying the permanent way and ballasting the line, whilst the road overbridges at Sunset and Kington were then expected to be available for traffic within a few weeks. Such momentum of the old Worcester to Aberystwyth

A well-known photograph reputedly showing work in progress on the alterations at Kington to enable the New Radnor extension to be built. It is likely that the workmen are cutting out a bed in order to divert the Langdale Brook.
Author's collection

ambitions that remained did eventually produce a railway between Bromyard and Leominster, but when Chambers referred to his 'laying out' of New Radnor station it was but a metaphorical corpse of the larger scheme. He was, however, so confident at the time that he said 'I beg to say that it will not be many months before this length also will be ready for opening.' The directors' comment that the line which 'it is expected ... will be completed by Christmas ... will open a new communication with the important Lime and Stone quarries of Old Radnor, and materially increase the traffic of the line' is more down to earth; had it not been for the quarries, the line would have been a total financial disaster. They were, in retrospect, the only realistic inducement for making the line, although they developed further with the building of the railway.

Despite the directors' confidence in February – 'The New Radnor Line is easy of construction ...' – difficulties evidently manifested themselves as, on 23rd October, Owen submitted for the sanction of the BOT a copy of the plans overlaid in red ink with more expedient alignments and gradients within the limit of deviation; the revised route was markedly different at the Kington end, but between Dolyhir and New Radnor the alterations were minimal. The BOT approved the revisions, which incorporated curves down to 11 and 12 chains radius, but stipulated that these should be provided with check rails, except on the approach to Kington where train speeds would be low as they neared the station. Indeed, early regulations for working the line stated:

'In consequence of there being a very heavy reverse curve soon after

leaving Kington in the direction of Radnor, it is necessary that Enginemen should use great caution in travelling until they have passed it. As there are several level crossings on this branch Enginemen are requested to keep a sharp lookout.'

Further, speed limits were *de rigueur* at several points along the line for the whole of its existence.

So the line was to be open by Christmas? In February 1875, the directors were only able to report that 'the works of the extension line to New Radnor have been continued with vigour ...', the Engineer confirming that:

'the whole of the earthworks, bridges, culverts and other works are, with some trifling exceptions, completed and the permanent way laid and ballasted to within a quarter of a mile of the termination of the line. The stations with the exception of New Radnor which is not yet commenced are in a forward state and now ready for the signalling.'

Interestingly enough, the physical connection at Kington was not approved by the GWR board until January 1875, the cost of £604 12s 6d being stipulated to be paid in advance. The share and loan capital had still not been taken up, and the building of New Radnor station not yet commenced, but otherwise the line was deemed to be fit for inspection by the Board of Trade. The writing was certainly on the wall for any extension to Rhayader (let alone Aberystwyth), for subsequent events show that, quite simply, the money was not there; indeed, Dolyhir station was built with the omission of one bay.

The line was required to be ready for Board of Trade inspection upon the requisite one month's notice of the intention to commence a train service being served; this was done on 1st June, and a second notice (on 23rd July) stated that it would be convenient for the inspection to take place within ten days of the 30th. The line was inspected by Col. Hutchinson, and his report, dated 6th August, read as follows:

'... I have inspected the New Radnor extension of the K & E. This line, which is single throughout with sidings at the stations, is 6m 47ch long. Land has been purchased and the overbridges constructed for a double line. It joins the line from Leominster to Kington at a new station which has been constructed at Kington, the other new stations being Stanner, Dolyhir and a temporary terminal station at New Radnor.

'The permanent way consists of wrot iron flat bottom rails weighing 72lbs per yard in length of about 22ft fished at the joints. The sleepers are rectangular 9ft by 11ins by 5ins, 8 to each 22ft rail; the rails are secured by fang bolts at the joints and centres and spikes intermediately. The ballast is of broken stone and gravel and stated to have a depth of 8in below the undersurface of the sleepers. The sharpest curve on the line has a radius of eleven chains, and the steepest gradient an incline of 1 in 50.

'There are three overbridges and ten underbridges, all having masonry abutments. Of the overbridges 2 have the platforms carried by wrot iron & one cast iron girders – largest span 29ft. Of the underbridges one has a stone arch and the remainder are spanned with wrot iron girders, the largest span being 15ft. Almost all these latter are over water.

'These bridges appear to have been all substantially constructed and to be standing well. They have sufficient theoretical strength & the iron underbridges gave moderate deflections under the passage of an engine.

'The fencing is of the most part post and wire, with portion of post and rail.

'There are 3 public road level crossings, provided with gates and lodges. There are no tunnels.

'The line has been carefully finished and the requirements are very few, being:

1. Locking bars for the facing points at Dolyhir and Kington Stations, the reversal of the weighting of the dead end points at New Radnor station and catch sidings at Kington station.

2. At Stanner Station the down end of the platform should terminate in a ramp.

3. Clocks visible from the platforms at all the stations.

4. A timber crane over the rails at Kington station should be removed.

5. The wall plate of the bridge at 0m. 58ch. requires packing.

'Subject to these requirements being completed I could have recommended the Board of Trade to have sanctioned the opening of the line but arrangements have not yet been made as to its working, the owning Co. having at present no rolling stock of their own.

'I must therefore report that by reason of incompleteness of the works and the absence of means for working the New Radnor extension line of the Kington and Eardisley Railway it cannot be opened for passenger traffic without danger to the public using the same.

'When working arrangements are completed the Co. shd. bear in mind that the mode of working cannot be by staff and ticket unless the block telegraph is provided.

'It will be desirable that only very moderate speed should be observed in running toward the reverse curves near Kington Station. I have etc.'

A notice postponing the opening for one month was issued on 9th August, the company replying on 9th September to say that the improvements had been done with the exception of the locking bars at Kington 'which are being done'. On the 10th, they gave an undertaking that the line would be worked only by a single engine in steam. The undertaking could not be sealed by the GW as all heads of departments, the Chairman and Secretary were on their vacations, but the BOT accepted an interim undertaking by the K & E and replied 'I think the opening may be allowed subject to the locking bars being speedily fixed ...'

The stage was therefore set for the usual jamboree, which took place (despite the short notice) on 25th September. The first train was crowded with holiday folk all bent upon a day's enjoyment at New Radnor, although the station was, in the very best railway tradition, some way from the community it purported to serve. Due to the short notice, there was an absence of flags, evergreens etc., but a hearty welcome was given, the cheers being heard far above the sharp crack of fog signals. The Kington Voluntary Band was soon in position as the last coach emptied, and the passengers marched towards the town to the sound of Christy's lively airs. The town was seemingly better prepared, and there was bunting over the shops. An outdoor procession at midday contained the carcass of a fine, fat ox drawn on a waggon; after the arrival of the second train, it was paraded through the town and given to the poor. A luncheon was held at the town hall, attended by 100 persons. The customary speeches were given by Sir Richard Green Price, Mr. Chambers and Mr. Cheese, these being followed by impromptu sports, which were kept up with unabated energy until the shadows of evening came. A fire-work display then took place, after which the company dispersed, having spent a most enjoyable day.

Col. Hutchinson made reference to a temporary station at New Radnor. In February 1875, the GWR had been asked to advance £14,000 in order that the line to New Radnor could be completed. However, the terms suggested by the K & E were unacceptable, and only after a fresh submission (in which the chairman and four directors of the company offered debentures as security) did the GWR approve, on the basis that repayment was made by 1st May 1877.

In September, therefore, New Radnor station was still incomplete. G. Wells Owen's rather beautiful design had to be abandoned in the light of the existing financial situation, and a simpler arrangement substituted. Perhaps the drawings for the lime works station could be used if the roof was made to look a little more dignified, and the pitch steepened? The goods shed was built even later.

From the outset, the line was worked by the GWR under an agreement that set a five-yearly pattern for renewal. The financial situation did not improve to any significant degree, and the K & E's requests for the GWR to purchase the company outright met with little interest. In the event, the GWR did eventually take over the K & E, in 1897, the powers being obtained by one of the private Acts of Parliament that railways obtained routinely in the course of their business.

The Great Western must have realised how light the traffic would be as, in 1890, the line was relaid using largely second hand materials. Some of the sleepers were new, but the rail and chairs had been in use elsewhere; the 21 ft rail lengths were laid upside down, using chairs with inside keys, the resultant track work lasting until just after the Great War.

CHAPTER TWO

A GREAT WESTERN
BRANCH LINE

A view eastwards through Kington station, with passenger trains crossing and the signal clear for the nearer train to depart to New Radnor. The sharp turnout was necessitated by the proximity of the bridge over the Langdale Brook to the platform end.

W. H. McKaig, courtesy E. P. Jobson

FOLLOWING its completion, the line settled down to a daily routine that was in effect uninterrupted by the subsequent change of ownership, for the Great Western had worked the line from the outset. As may be expected, the New Radnor line was integrated to a large degree within the overall working pattern of all the 'Kington branches', with traffic to and from Presteign and Eardisley interconnecting with the Radnor trains on the Leominster services; Kington was naturally the hub of those operations.

The early timetable, for November 1875, shows five trains in each direction over the branch, with the first up and last down services being 'mixed', conveying both passenger and goods traffic. The line was initially worked by 'Train Staff', (triangular in shape); other instructions relating to the operation of the branch were reproduced with the timetable, as may be seen, and are mainly concerned with the formation of the trains. Information as to the actual make-up of these early services is naturally sparse, but trains would probably have consisted of a tank engine with four-wheel passenger and goods stock.

By 1902, the branch services had altered somewhat, with the daily passenger trains being reduced to three in each direction, one of which ('mixed') also handled important goods traffic; there was also a fourth return service, between Kington and New Radnor, on Saturday nights only. This pattern of traffic remained much the same until the outbreak of the Second World War, although the Saturday night trip does not seem to have survived the Great War.

The branch now boasted a through goods service, leaving Leominster at 9.5 a.m. and arriving at New Radnor, 12.10 p.m.; after fifteen minutes at the terminus, the engine departed with the return service. There was also provision for two 'conditional' (run when required) return goods trips from Kington to New Radnor, leaving

KINGTON AND NEW RADNOR RAILWAY.

Miles.	Single Line. Worked by Train Staff.	DOWN TRAINS.											
		1	2	3	4	5							
		Pass.	Pass.	Pass.	Pass.	Ps.&Gds.							
		A.M.	A.M.	A.M.	P.M.	P.M.							
.....	**Kington** ....dep.	6 45	10 32	11 32	2 20	5 5	•	•	•	•	•	•	•
2¾	Stanner	6 54	10 41	11 41	2 29	5 18	••	••	••	••	••	••	••
4¾	Dolhier	6 59	10 46	11 46	2 34	5 28	•••	•••	•••	•••	•••	•••	•••
6½	**New Radnor** ...arr.	7 5	10 52	11 52	2 40	5 35	•	•	•	•	•	•	•

Miles.		Pass. and G'ds.	UP TRAINS.										
		A.M.	A.M.	A.M.	P.M.	P.M.							
...	**New Radnor** ...dep.	7 20	10 57	11 57	2 50	6 55	•	•	•	•	•	•	•
2¾	Dolhier .... „	7 27	11 3	12 3	2 57	7 2	••	••	••	••	••	••	••
3¾	Stanner .... „	7 32	11 8	12 8	3 2	7 7	•••	•••	•••	•••	•••	•••	•••
6½	**Kington**............arr.	7 40	11 15	12 15	3 10	7 15	•	•	•	•	•	•	•

SPECIAL INSTRUCTIONS.

The Line will be worked by Train Staff, and no Train or Engine must be allowed to run over the Single Line without the Staff.

SHAPE OF STAFF.

TRIANGULAR.

All Trains must have a Break Van as the last vehicle in the Train.

All Passenger Trains must have a Break to every four vehicles. In ascending the Inclines, each Break-vehicle must be so placed in the Train as to have only three vehicles in front of it.

The speed of any Train must not exceed 25 miles per hour.

The Guard must ride in the last Break Van on the Train.

No Goods Train must exceed 16 loaded Waggons, and must be provided with sufficient Break power—not less than two good and efficient Breaks to every three Waggons. In ascending Inclines, if there should happen to be two Break Vans, one must be placed in the rear and the other in the middle of the Train, and a Guard must ride in each.

N.B.—As there are several level crossings on this Branch Enginemen are requested to keep a sharp look-out.

In consequence of there being a very heavy reverse curve soon after leaving Kington in the direction of Radnor, it is necessary that Enginemen should use great caution in travelling until they have passed it.

ENGINE WHISTLES.

KINGTON.

Trains going into Kington Old Yard are required to give .... 1 whistle.
Trains approaching Kington for New Radnor, and *vice versa* .... 2 whistles.

Taken from Working Timetable for November 1875.

the former at 7.0 a.m. and 8.0 p.m., returning from Radnor at 7.45 a.m. and 8.45 p.m. Yet another 'conditional' service was allowed for in the afternoons, but only between Kington and Dolyhir.

In that year, a clear indication of engine power on the branch may be gained from the allocations in the area;

Leominster

'517' class 0–4–2T	574, 1430, 1437, 1470
'1501' class 0–6–0ST	1809
'2021' class 0–6–0ST	2036, 2037

Kington

'2021' class 0–6–0ST	2027, 2035

The New Radnor extension, as indeed the whole of the Kington branch, was dominated by the activities of the Old Radnor Co. In addition to its lime and stone traffic, that company had a near-monopoly of the all-important coal trade. However, Stanner had a coal merchant – Walter Morgan. He was reputed to have around ten wagons, four of which were hired from the Birmingham RC & W Co. These were all 8 ton capacity vehicles; No. 1 entered service on 2nd November 1903, No. 2 on 22nd November 1904, No. 3 on 6th November 1906, whilst No. 5 was hired by an agreement dated 1st December 1917. No photographs of his wagons have yet been discovered.

It is believed that he was eventually bought out by the Old Radnor company. New Radnor also housed an 'independent' coal merchant, but again no further details have yet come to light.

The passenger train programme of 1911 shows the branch to have been operated with four-coach trains of six-wheel stock, thus:

Worcester set:	8.15 a.m. Worcester to New Radnor
	10.55 a.m. New Radnor to Worcester
	2.40 p.m. Worcester to New Radnor
	5.50 p.m. New Radnor to Worcester

The formation was: (six-wheel) Brake Third, Compo, Third, Van. These services operated via the Bromyard line, and it is possible that the engines worked through with the coaches (at least, on one of the trips).

Leominster set:	1.0 p.m. Leominster to New Radnor
	2.20 p.m. New Radnor to Worcester
	7.50 p.m. Worcester to Leominster

Again, the formation was: Brake Third, Compo, Third, Van (all six-wheel stock).

The through working between Worcester and New Radnor was almost certainly dictated by operating convenience rather than a commercial necessity to connect the little town with that city. Nevertheless, it was a slightly

A view of Dolyhir, thought to date from the 1890s. Even this small station could muster a fair-sized staff group, including two with shunters' poles. The man with his foot up on the bench has in his hand the train staff; he is holding it by the key used to unlock ground frames working points connected to the running line.   *Courtesy Rev. D. A. Tipper*

A view of the locomotive shed at Leominster, with a train approaching from the direction of Kington Junction, viewed from the occupation footbridge at the north end of Leominster station. The double junction in the foreground led to the platforms serving the Bromyard line. The corn mill on the left once had its own private siding running behind the PW hut. It was opened in 1867 and trailed into the southbound main line beneath the footbridge. The shed replaced one immediately to the south of the passenger station complex and provided the loco used on the New Radnor passenger service. The building in the right foreground was almost certainly converted from the brick base of the original Bromyard Junction signal box.

W. H. McKaig, courtesy E. P. Jobson

Two inhabitants of Leominster shed during the early years of this century are here depicted in early 1900s condition albeit at different locations.

Author's collection

Leominster Station.

Leominster station, looking south (c.1910) with the signal box and LNWR pattern signal dominating the scene. The main line platforms are on the right, with those serving the branch to Bromyard and Worcester in the centre. The platform on the extreme left served the New Radnor trains as well as the Bromyard branch.

Author's collection

Early views of the branch are scarce. This one of New Radnor, believed to have been taken c.1920, shows the usual wooden fence which was removed before the 1930s.   *Lens of Sutton*

Arrival at New Radnor, Edwardian style. The sleeper-built platform made for easier loading of baggage onto one's trap. The black painted end of the station building shows up well here.
W. H. McKaig, courtesy Lens of Sutton

unusual situation, and of some benefit to the inhabitants of New Radnor!

Before the Great War, the daily goods to New Radnor was scheduled to run from Hereford, departing at 8.25 a.m. behind an o–6–o engine (possibly one of Hereford's 'Armstrong Goods'); this conveyed traffic 'for the Kington and New Radnor Branches'. On Mondays, Wednesdays and Fridays this train terminated at Dolyhir, and any important through traffic for New Radnor on those days was detached at Kington, and forwarded on the following 1.0 p.m. Leominster (mixed) service. If traffic warranted, the goods was extended through to New Radnor from Dolyhir.

Engine allocation on the branch in 1914 remained much as in 1902, with '517' class o–4–2Ts and '2021' o–6–oSTs dominant. Kington still had a pair of saddle tanks.

In 1922, passenger services remained at three trains in each direction, again using the four-coach six-wheel formations, now called 'S' Sets. The workings were identical to those tabulated for 1911.

From about 1922, Kington shed's allocation alternated between o–4–2T and o–6–oT classes, but had settled down to '517s' by 1925. At around this time, the o–6–oTs seem to have largely moved away from Leominster too, with o–4–2Ts now taking the lion's share of the workings.

It is tempting to think that New Radnor, being rather remote from Paddington, escaped the attention of

W. H. McKaig, courtesy Lens of Sutton

officialdom. However, following much effort by the local populace to bring about an extension of the line, the case was taken up by the local authorities. In March 1923, the Kington UDC resolved to petition the Great Western to extend the branch into Central Wales. The pressure was indeed taken seriously by the GWR who, in August of that year, authorised three possible routes to be surveyed (south-westwards to Builth, westwards to Newbridge-on-

The inter-war atmosphere is evoked in this 1929 view of a New Radnor to Leominster train drifting into Kington on an exceptionally hot day. The sign erected amongst the lineside allotments, adjacent to the locomotive shed, was a 'whistle' board. The locomotive is one of the '3571' class 0—4—2Ts.

J. E. Kite

Another inter-war view, c.1930, this time of New Radnor. The signs advertising the *Daily Telegraph* suspended beneath the station nameboards were evident on many GWR stations at this time. Round timber was a regular source of traffic for the otherwise quiet goods yard behind the passenger platform.   *Photographer unknown*

Wye via Llandrindod Wells, and north-westwards to Rhayader). On 25th August, Felix Pole (General Manager), James Milne (Assistant General Manager), C.B. Collett (Chief Mechanical Engineer) and R.H. Nicholls (Superintendent of the Line) arrived in New Radnor by motor car, and after viewing the station left for Llandrindod Wells, where they stayed the night. The distinguished quartet then spent two days motoring in the Aberystwyth area.

The estimated cost of the extension was given as £1¾ million, and later in the year they indicated that 'on a purely commercial standpoint the cost of construction cannot be justified, even though there is no doubt that it would encourage local development of the area.' A scarcely surprising conclusion.

A report on all GWR branch lines, made in 1925, recommended certain economies; those affecting the New Radnor line were:

1. Replacement of the electric train key between Kington and New Radnor by a wooden train staff (saving £20 p.a.)
2. Withdrawal of station staff at Stanner (saving £200 p.a.)
3. Dispensing with the porter/signalman at New Radnor (saving £125 p.a.)

These recommendations were eventually implemented in inverse order of necessity. The train staff replacement was approved by the board in 1926 and an undertaking given to the MOT, whilst the uniformed staff changes took place in 1938. Stanner became unstaffed in that year, as per the recommendations, although it was the station master (and not the porter/signalman) that was removed from New Radnor.

Until 1938, staffed by a station master and a porter, New Radnor was a haven of peace! With the proximity of a number of large estates, it could be a very agreeable position for a suitably-minded station master, though it was not to everyone's taste. In the spring of 1935 when the station master at New Radnor, H. Harries, was moved to Tetbury, he was replaced by C.P. (Percy) Cotton who was promoted from a similar post at Lyonshall. However, some fifteen months later, station master Cotton was glad to move on to Awre Junction, being replaced by R.S. (Stan) Freeman, from Cinderford.

Mr. Cotton's wife was a keen gardener, and her efforts are evident from photographs taken in the latter 'thirties. His first experience of New Radnor was in connection with the station master's house, which was in such a poor state that he refused to live in it, taking lodgings elsewhere in the town instead. An extensive dispute with the Wolverhampton Estates Office resulted in the house being refurbished, with a new kitchen and toilet. The house was not the usual GWR-built structure, but one in the village purchased in 1920 for the sum of £160; the erection of a standard house had been approved in 1913, but was not built.

In the late summer of 1938, W.R. (Bill) Williams moved up from Almeley (on the Eardisley branch) to Kington as porter/guard, at which time station master Stan Freeman and his porter, G.E. Phillips, both moved away from New Radnor as part of the rationalisation proposals. Bill's typical day would begin with booking on at Kington at 8.30 a.m. to work on the 9.0 a.m. departure to Eardisley (which connected with a train for Hay) and the 10.2 a.m. return (until the closure of the line in 1940). This then

A general view of the station, probably taken after the departure of Percy Cotton. His garden is beginning to look a little wild.
Lens of Sutton

This contemporary view is looking back along the platform. The protecting fixed distant signal can just be seen, and the ground frame is also visible.
Lens of Sutton

gave him a few minutes at Kington to catch the 9.50 a.m. Leominster train to New Radnor. On arrival he would unlock the station and work there until 6.0 p.m., when he would secure the station before leaving on the 6.5 p.m. train, as far as Kington.

During the early 'thirties, two members of the '3571' class 0–4–2Ts appeared on the line, Nos. 3573 and 3574, having been transferred from the Wolverhampton Division. No. 3574 in particular was associated with the branch, and was known to be shedded at Kington during both 1937 and 1940, as well as having spells at Leominster between 1930 and 1934.

The '3571s' were, by the mid-'thirties, getting a bit long in the tooth, and were gradually replaced by the new Collett '58XX' class 0–4–2 tanks, the first pair of which (Nos. 5807 and 5814) arrived at Kington during 1934. By 1938, both Leominster and Kington had a pair, with three others (including the spares) at Worcester. This balance remained largely unaltered until the withdrawal of passenger services on the branch.

Passenger stock had also changed by this time; the 6-wheel stock had been withdrawn, and replaced by bogie van third & brake compo combinations. This stock (one Worcester and one Leominster set) worked in exactly the same way as in 1911, though minor changes to timings had occurred in the meantime. The coaches were mainly elderly GWR clerestory stock, but former Cambrian Railway vehicles also found their way onto the branch. The 1933-built bow-ended 'B' sets replaced these during the mid-1930s.

The goods yard at New Radnor was only lightly used, as most of the traffic was quite able to be carried in the van sections of the passenger trains. However, generally one or two wagons or vans arrived on the goods each day.

Regular traffic had included milk for the Cadbury factory at Ford Bridge (near Leominster), but after 1947 this was taken direct in road tankers. Other traffic included bales of straw which, destined for paper-making at Ross-on-Wye, were usually loaded into open wagons and sheeted over. The loading process had to be carefully organised as the bales were heavy, and despite the attention given, a near-fatal accident did once occur. An occasional cattle truck might put in an appearance in later years, whilst potatoes (for stock feeding) were also loaded in the yard. An Old Radnor Trading Company wagon would also periodically visit the station.

New Radnor's own coal merchant experienced much competition from businesses in Rhayader and Knighton as well as from the Old Radnor Trading Co., and he could take up to a month to dispose of the contents of his coal wagon. Bill Williams took pity on him, and never charged demurrage!

The 'village shop' in New Radnor was run by another Williams, and 'sold everything': their supplies arrived by train, and were unloaded and stored in the goods shed

No. 3573 was a visitor to the branch during the 1930s.

J. E. Kite

pending delivery. Another porter, Roy Lewis, recalled that on alternate weeks, he would travel to New Radnor by the first train and spend the day delivering parcels around the locality with the aid of a wheelbarrow, returning to Kington on the last train.

With the introduction of the 'National Emergency' timetables in 1939, passenger services were again reduced, this time two trains in each direction, giving a mid-morning and an early-evening train over the branch.

The '58XXs' were joined by 0–6–0 tanks of the '74XX' class on the odd service during the war and, despite the 'lightly-laid' nature of the line, '57XX' class engines also appeared from time to time.

During the war years, New Radnor became an extremely busy station handling timber for a nearby Forestry Commission camp; 7 or 8 wagon loads of pit props were dispatched daily. With a Royal Engineers establishment in the vicinity, which brought the movement of army and other personnel, the passenger balance often exceeded £1,000 per month. There was no shortage of overtime then!

Bill Williams discovered a bat living in a crevice behind the firebuckets on the end wall of the station, and in quieter moments would impale dead flies from the booking office windows onto bent paper clips, and feed these to the lodger – a crunching sound would confirm that the free meal was appreciated!

On one occasion during the War German bombers (returning from a raid on Liverpool) jettisoned a landmine, which exploded on the Smatcher. Curiously, the blast caused the windows opening onto the platform to be blown in, but windows facing the hill were sucked out. The damage was temporarily repaired with a plastic sheet reinforced with gauze. It is ironic that the remotest part of the Kington branches was the only section to be subjected to enemy action.

There was also a break-in at the station, attributed to soldiers, and an immediate visit was made by the auditor to check cash and tickets.

During September, on unofficial 'market' in elderberries was held, the station scales being used to weight the

NEW RADNOR, KINGTON, PRESTEIGN AND LEOMINSTER BRANCHES.

UP TRAINS.

WEEK DAYS ONLY.

Miles (from Kington)				Ruling Gradient 1 in	Time Allowances for Ordinary Freight Trains. See page 5.			STATIONS.	Mixed.	Pass.	Pass.
M.	C.				Point to Point times. Mins.	Allow for Stop. Mins.	Allow for Start. Mins.		B dep. a.m.	B dep. a.m.	B dep. a.m.
				L				NEW RADNOR ... dep.			10 50
1	71				4	2	1	Stop Board ...			10 56
3	39			50 F	2			Dolyhir ...			11 0
3	53			50 F	3			Stanner ...			
5	45				3			Stop Board ...			11 6
6	43			60 F	4		1	KINGTON {arr. dep.	7 21	10 28	11 X 9
				132 R					7 25	10 31	11 X 12
8	23	1	60					Titley ... {dep. arr.	7 26	10 32	11 13
				44 R			1	Forge Crossing ... dep.		10 35	
								PRESTEIGN ... arr.		10 44	
10	36			132 R	10		1	Marston Halt and Siding ... dep.	7 32		11 19
12	22			106 F	9			Pembridge ...	7 37		11 24
15	79			208 F	9			Kingsland ...	7 46		11 33
19	11	7	37	176 R	5			Kington Junction ...	CS		CS
20	25			291 F	2		1	LEOMINSTER ... arr.	7 55		11 40

STATIONS.	Mixed.	Hereford Cattle.	Pass.	Freight.	Mixed.	Pass.	Pass.
	B SX RR dep. a.m.	K RR THO arr. dep.	B dep. p.m.	K SO arr. dep. p.m.	B dep. p.m.	B dep. p.m.	B dep. p.m.
NEW RADNOR ... dep.				12 25	6 5		7 15
Stop Board ...				12 30	6 11		7 20
Dolyhir ...				12 35	6 15		7 29
Stanner ...				12 50			CS
Stop Board ...				1 8	6 21		7 2
KINGTON {arr. dep.	11 50		2 10	2 20	6X27		7 36
	CS	6 5	2 12		6 30		
Titley {dep. arr.	1 10	C S	2X15		6 32		
	1X15						
Forge Crossing ... dep.	1 20						
PRESTEIGN ... arr.		6 41	2 42	3 40			
Marston Halt and Siding ... dep.	1 25		2 21	C R	6 38		
Pembridge ...	1 36		2 26	3 38	6 43		
Kingsland ...			2 35	3 38	6 52		
Kington Junction ...	12 10		CS	CS	CS		
LEOMINSTER ... arr.	CS	7 5			7 2		

R—To stop whether required for traffic purposes or not.

Traffic to and from Marston Siding (Pembridge). Traffic to or from this Siding will be dealt with by the 12.25 p.m. Freight Train ex New Radnor. The Guard must hand a memorandum each day to the Station Master at Pembridge shewing :—

The numbers and contents to be shewn in each case and the labels of the inwards wagons to be attached to the memorandum.

1st—What wagons he has put off at the Siding.
2nd—What wagons he has picked up at the Siding.

3rd—If he has not attached or detached any wagons, a Nil memorandum must be given up, and he must shew on the Nil memorandum the total number of wagons there are in the Siding, Penbridge will advise Kington what wagons they may send to the Siding daily, and also consignees.

ENGINE ROUTES—NEW 0-4-2 TANK ENGINES, 14XX AND 58XX CLASSES.

Subject to the observance of Permanent Restrictions of Speed, it has been agreed to the above engines working over the following Branches :—

New Radnor, Presteign.

LEOMINSTER, KINGTON, NEW RADNOR AND PRESTEIGN BRANCHES.

Leominster and Kington Single Line worked by Electric Train Staff between Kington Junction (Leominster) and Kington.

Kington and New Radnor Single Line worked by Train Staff and only one Engine in steam at a time (or two coupled together) between Kington and New Radnor.

Crossing Stations.—Kington Junction, Pembridge, Titley and Kington. All Trains must stop at Kington. Two Passenger Trains conveying Passengers must not under ordinary circumstances cross at Pembridge, nor must Passenger Trains conveying Passengers be allowed to cross in the Loop at Pembridge.

Titley & Presteign Single Line worked by Train Staff, and only one Engine in steam at a time, or two or more coupled together.

DOWN TRAINS.

WEEK DAYS ONLY.

Mile Post Mileage from Kington Jct.		Distance.		Ruling Gradient 1 in	Time Allowances for Ordinary Freight Trains. See page 5.		STATIONS.	Freight.	Mixed.	Pass.
M.	C.	M.	C.		Point to Point times. Mins.	Allow for Start. Mins.		K dep. a.m.	B dep. a.m.	B dep. a.m.
				291 R			LEOMINSTER ... dep.	8 5	6 18	9 50
—†				L	2	1	Kington Junction ...	C S	CS	CS
3	72			176 R	9	1	Kingsland ...	8 17	6 29	9 59
7	49			208 R	9	1	Pembridge ...	9 5	6 38	10 7
9	40			106 R		1	Marston Halt & Siding ...	9 30	6 45	10 13
		4	7	45 R			PRESTEIGN ... dep.			
		5	57				Forge Crossing ... {arr. dep.	C R	6 52	
11	48	7	37	80 R	12	1	Titley {arr. dep.	10 5	6 53	10 56
				80 R	14		{dep. arr.	C R	6 57	11 8
13	28			132 R	12	1	KINGTON {arr. dep.	11 30		11 X14
16	32			60 R	5		Stanner ...	12 7		11 17
17	66			50 R	6		Dolyhir ...			
19				50 R		1	NEW RADNOR ... arr.	11 X15 W120		10 45

STATIONS.	Freight SX	Mixed.	Mixed SO	Pass.	Mixed.	Pass.
	RR dep.	dep. p.m.	dep.	B dep. p.m.	dep. p.m.	B dep. p.m.
LEOMINSTER ... dep.	11.45 a.m. Hereford Cattle Empties. RR ThO	12A38 12 48	1 55	4 55	5X24	9 35
Kington Junction ...	C S	12 53	2 6	5 9	5 26	9 36
Kingsland ...	C186S	1 1	2 11	5 12	5 29	9 14
Pembridge ...	CS	1 9	2X17	5 18	5 34	9 22
Marston Halt & Siding ...	CS	1 10	2 22		5 41	9Q29
PRESTEIGN ... dep.					5 45	
Forge Crossing ... arr.	CS				5 51	
Titley {arr. dep.	1 0	1 17 X	6 0	6 16	6 0	
	1 25	1 20	6 11	6 17	6 11	9 36
KINGTON {arr. dep.	1 30	1X24		6X22		9 39
Stanner ...	1 43					
Dolyhir ...						10 39
NEW RADNOR ... arr.						10 45

A—Advertised Leominster depart 12 35 p.m.

W—RR between Dolyhir and New Radnor

Q—Time allowed for Guard to extinguish lights when necessary.

†—34 ch Leominster to Kington Junction.

6.18 a.m. Mixed Leominster to Kington.

To be so formed as to avoid the necessity of an assistant Guard from Leominster. The Passenger Brake third must be found next in front of the Guard's Van and be used for Mails only, under the control of the Guard.

Taken from GWR Service Timetable for 6th October 1947 until further notice.

Wolverhampton-built '3571' class 0—4—2T No. 3574 plus 1933-built 'B' set, was from that year until 1947, the regular branch train formation. It is shown here at Titley Junction on a Worcester—New Radnor train via Bromyard and Leominster, on 27th September 1947.

R. J. Buckley

baskets, for which privilege, payment to the 'station staff' was made in fruit. American troops were billeted at Harpton Court, and their generosity ensured that porter Williams was never short of the necessities of life, such as cigarettes, sugar, bacon and butter. Despite the war and the following austerity, Bill Williams claimed that they were the best days of his working life, growing potatoes opposite the platform, feeding the bat, and listening to the cricket scores on his crystal set, which he had rigged up in the office. In the summer months, it was also possible to spend an hour or two hiking on the surrounding hills, from which he often viewed the approach of visiting authority in the form of the car-borne District Inspector!

The train crews also took advantage of the area's wildlife. Freddie Gardner would regularly stop his train between Dolyhir and New Radnor, where the line was out of sight of any kind of authority, in order to lay a rabbit wire. This would be duly inspected on subsequent trips when his dinner would usually be assured. Pheasants were bred at Harpton Court, and became so tame that they would sit on the boundary fence posts; they became fair game (in more than one sense) for a carefully aimed lump of coal. They were collected on the return journey. Cock pheasants were often found in the yard at New Radnor, where any fights were usually broken up by the use of a shunting pole! Goods trains did not always run through to New Radnor, especially if there were no wagons to be dealt with, the engine running round its train at Dolyhir; nevertheless, the crew would often 'fancy a trip' to the terminus if only to enjoy a bit of sport on the way!

The New Radnor branch was susceptible to weather problems with the onset of winter. If a snowstorm occurred on a Saturday night or a Sunday, the station masters were

required to consider the information passed to them by the line's gangers and, if necessary, run a light engine from Kington to New Radnor and back to Leominster before the first booked train on Monday, to ensure that traffic could be kept moving.

However, the severe winter of 1947 was especially memorable, with the frost breaking off branches, and snowdrifts mounting up in the cuttings. The bank between Dolyhir and New Radnor was always bad in these circumstances, and this particular year was no exception. Bill Williams remembers walking back to Kington on one occasion when the train could not get through. Leaving New Radnor station at 4 p.m., he walked through the gathering darkness along the track as far as Stanner, where he took the road thence to Kington, arriving at 10.0 p.m. It was not unknown, in such difficult circumstances, for passengers to be conveyed by the goods train, where they would ride in the brake van comforted by the welcome heat from the guard's stove.

The New Radnor extension seems to have been relatively accident-free, though on one occasion, when a solitary passenger was being given a lift in a GWR delivery lorry, the driver managed to hit the arch of the last bridge under the line before New Radnor. To add to his discomfort, he was rebuked for carrying an unauthorised member of the public, who would not have been insured!

One potential source of accidents was the run-round loop at New Radnor, where the 'station-end' point was operated by a lever alongside. After the loco had uncoupled and moved clear of that point, it was then thrown and often followed by some nifty footwork on the part of the porter/guard to reach the ground frame at the far end of the layout before the engine. The turnout at the entrance to the loop was locked by a key on the

The one and only Freddie Gardner and his fireman Ken Chapman awaiting the right of way for Leominster, c.1949. Freddie had no teeth, was an extremely fast driver and was once witnessed hanging out of the cab of his loco and whipping it with a stick as though it was a horse.   *R. H. Jobson*

train staff which the porter collected from the engine on arrival. With the porter riding on the steps, the loco would then proceed along the run-round as far as the catch point (protected by a ground signal), where the porter would dismount and make his way on foot to the ground frame. Having unlocked, he would pull the facing point lock and loop entry/catch point levers so that the loco could complete running round its train. However, there were busy times during the war when crews unfamiliar with the procedure came to Radnor, and if Bill Williams was otherwise engaged, the guard would take his place and the existence of the catch point was overlooked. There were several derailments of locos, at that position! The following is an official report of one such incident on 22nd October 1945:

Description of Occurrence
    The 4.55 p.m. passenger ex Leominster arrived at New Radnor at 5.54 p.m. and the Fireman took the wooden train staff to operate the points to permit of the engine running round the train via the Loop. The Engine No. 4678 (Driver T.W. Jones of Leominster) negotiated the points from platform to loop and came to a stand well clear of the Loop Catch Points.
    The Fireman then proceeded to the Ground Frame and operated Levers Nos. 3 and 4 which control the points via Loop to Yard, leaving the Catch Point still open. The Fireman then shouted to the Driver to come ahead, which the latter did, and the engine became derailed three wheels at the Catch Point and after travelling a further 23 yards came to rest.
    The Hereford Breakdown Vans were ordered at 6.40 p.m., left Hereford at 8.4 p.m., arrived at New Radnor at 9.45 p.m., engine rerailed 11.30 p.m., Breakdown Vans left at midnight.
    A car was hired to convey the Fireman with train staff to Kington where he arrived at 6.40 p.m.
    The Kington Station Master left Kington with another engine at 6.45 p.m., arrived at New Radnor at 7.0 p.m., drew the coaches clear and left for Kington at 7.11 p.m., arriving at 7.26 p.m.
    The necessary repairs were completed and normal working resumed at noon on October 23rd.

Trains delayed and extent of delay
    6.5 p.m. New Radnor to Leominster delayed 65 minutes.

A bus was obtained in lieu of the following services:
    10.28 a.m. Kington to New Radnor   } October
    10.52 a.m. New Radnor to Kington   } 23rd

One part of the extension was built on land leased from the Harpton Court Estate, and a condition was imposed such that trains were obliged to stop, and give way to the local hunt should it happen to be in full cry. This was not an uncommon arrangement elsewhere, especially in the early days.

Just after the war, cattle which had been put out onto 'The Smatcher' had to be loaded into cattle wagons at New Radnor. They had become quite wild and had to be 'roped' in order to restrain them before they could be loaded up.

The popular Radnor Fair was quite a large event, and was held at the end of each October. On the first day, sheep were the subject of attention, whilst horses and cattle would have a day to themselves. The GWR would send a shunting horse to New Radnor (in a horsebox) for the duration of the fair.

Whilst New Radnor would not normally see many tourists, one favourite outing for Kington folk would be to take a train there, and then head for the surrounding hills in order to pick whinberries. This activity gradually died out with the introduction of conifers in an afforestation programme of so much of Radnor Forest.

Bill Williams retired in 1949 just two years before the branch was closed.

In the final years of the New Radnor line, the service remained at two passenger trains, and a goods (to Dolyhir, but extended to Radnor when required). An interesting glimpse of the final years was recorded by an RCTS member in January 1949, published in the *Railway Observer*.

Engine	Turn
No. 5817	4.55 p.m. Leominster–New Radnor Passenger
	6.5 p.m. New Radnor–Leominster Passenger
No. 7420	8.5 a.m. Leominster–New Radnor Freight
	12.25 p.m. New Radnor–Leominster Freight
No. 7437	9.50 a.m. Leominster–New Radnor Passenger
	10.50 a.m. New Radnor–Leominster Passenger

In the summer of 1951 the New Radnor branch was closed to passenger traffic, an early casualty in the run-down of the whole British railway system, which began tentatively in the inter-war period and reached its climax in the mid-'sixties. Shortly afterwards the goods services between Dolyhir and New Radnor were also withdrawn and the line between those places abandoned; the telephone (bus circuit No. 1000) between Kington and New Radnor was recovered. Goods traffic between Kington and Dolyhir, regularly handled by '74XX' 0–6–0PTs, continued until the mid-'fifties when it, too, was withdrawn.

A view of the south end of Leominster station, taken from the over-bridge carrying the Worcester road, showing the extensive goods yard and water crane. A train from the direction of Worcester and Bromyard is approaching the branch platforms at Leominster station in June 1951.
Derek Clayton

Auto-coaches were used for a short while on the Kington branch during the 1950s after the New Radnor extension had been closed. One of these can be seen here occupying the platform used by the New Radnor and Bromyard trains, in June 1951.
Derek Clayton

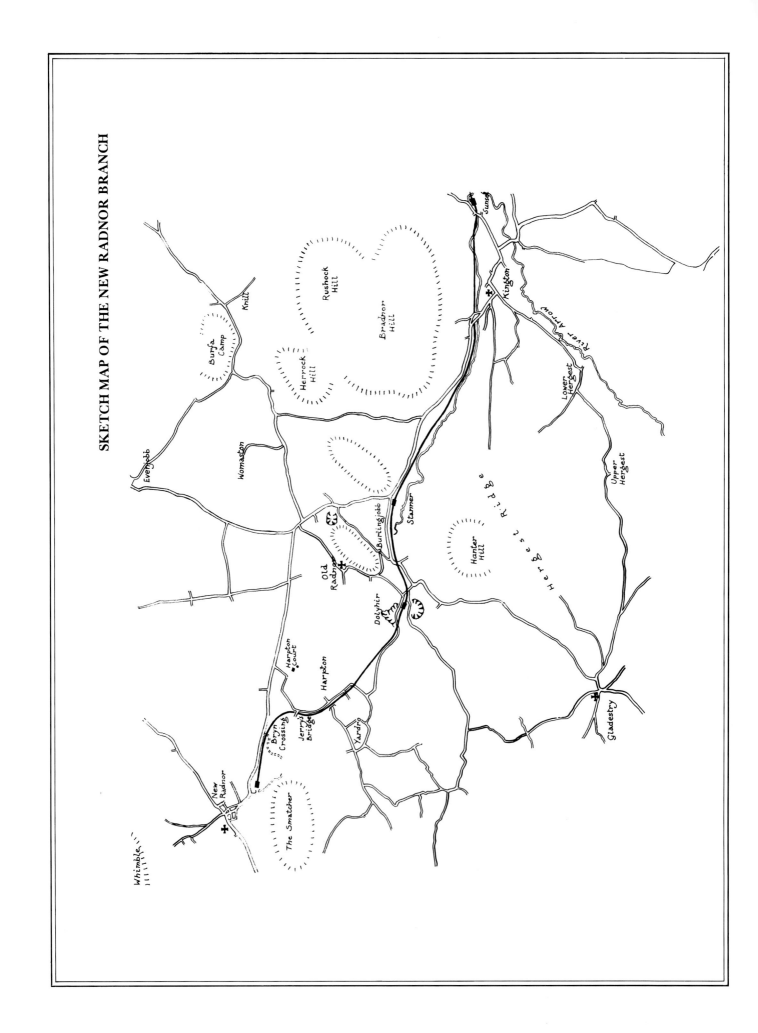

SKETCH MAP OF THE NEW RADNOR BRANCH

Whimble

New Radnor

The Smatcher

Bryn Crossing

Jerry's Bridge

Yardro

Harpton

Harpton Court

Old Radnor

Dolyhir

Stanner

Burlingjobb

Womaston

Evenjobb

Knill

Burfa Camp

Herrock Hill

Rushock Hill

Bradnor Hill

Hanter Hill

Herbest Ridge

Upper Hergest

Lower Hergest

River Arrow

Kington

Sunset

Gladestry

CHAPTER THREE

ALONG THE LINE

ANY significant development of extant railway facilities invariably involved some degree of redesigning, most especially if a line were to be extended beyond an existing terminus for which provision had not originally been made. Such was the case at Kington, where the building of the New Radnor extension had necessitated the construction of a new, through passenger station to the north of the old L & K terminus. As already explained, the passenger portion of the old station was then incorporated into the goods facilities. Beyond Kington, the line for the most part followed river valleys, and the first river crossing occurred immediately beyond the platforms of the new station. This first stretch of line was overlooked by the brooding hills of Bradnor to the north and Hergest ridge to the south, and was particularly beautiful. Despite the sinuous nature of the line, it was laid to fairly reasonable gradients (1 in 50 being the steepest), though the railway was in virtually continuous climb between Kington

A view of Kington station, on 19th August 1948, from the down starting signal, looking east towards Leominster, showing the branch locomotive backing onto the 'B' set in the down platform and a Dean Goods shunting the goods yard. The existence of a long headshunt to the yard allowed these operations to proceed simultaneously. *L. E. Copeland*

The eastern approach to Kington station on 19th August 1948. The layout here was remodelled in 1905, with a new running line on the left, and the former running line on the right converted into a long headshunt. The pointwork allowed flexibility in working, but was a rather expensive luxury. The Langdale Brook passed under the railway amid all the connections.

L. E. Copeland

Another view of the eastern throat, from ground level, on 19th August 1948, with the 1905-built signal box on the left. The left-hand bracket signal applied to the up line, whilst the one in the centre applied to up direction movement from the down platform line, allowing Leominster-bound trains to depart from the down platform (see below). This was especially convenient since the down platform was nearest the station buildings and there was no footbridge, but could only be utilised by trains starting from Kington, not through trains from New Radnor.   *L. E. Copeland*

This panorama of Kington station, like the photo on page 26, was taken from the centre bracket signal in the view above, on 19th August 1948. The alignment into the former passenger station (now part of the goods yard) and the manner in which the new station for the New Radnor extension was built alongside, is evident here. This picture also shows the water tower away to the right, adjacent to the river which looped round the station between the bridges at the east and west ends.   *L. E. Copeland*

KINGTON STATION

$170\frac{1}{2}$

Kington station, prior to the 1905 remodelling of the east end of the layout.
Lens of Sutton

Links 100 50 0 1 2 3 4 5

The west end of Kington station on 19th August 1948, showing the changes in the scene since the turn of the century (see page 1) including the new coach body in the foreground and the awning to the goods shed. *L. E. Copeland*

Looking towards Sunset Bridge, from which the previous photo was taken, this view on 19th August 1948 shows the location of the engine shed at Kington, way out beyond the road overbridge. Originally constructed of timber, the bridge was built to double line dimensions. *L. E. Copeland*

Beyond the road bridge the line was on a curve so sharp as to require a permanent speed restriction. The shed housed two (latterly one) locos used on the Presteign and Eardisley branches. 19th August 1948.

L. E. Copeland

After leaving Kington, the line entered a narrow valley between Bradnor Hill to the north and Hergest Ridge to the south. The route of the horse-drawn tramway can be seen to the left of the river in this view looking towards Kington.   *Courtesy Allan Lloyd*

Looking back to Kington again and the bridge in the previous view.   *Courtesy Allan Lloyd*

Stanner station viewed shortly after the installation of the second siding in 1914.

L & GRP, cty. David & Charles

A late 1930s view of Stanner, looking towards Kington. The ground frame on the right contained the levers to work the siding points and facing point lock, which was released by a key on the single line staff.   *Lens of Sutton*

and the summit, about half a mile to the west of Dolyhir. In the initial section, the line rubbed shoulders with the river, road, and track bed of the now-defunct tramway.

After some two miles, the valley opened out and the first intermediate station, Stanner, was reached. This was truly diminutive, the building being constructed of stone and slate, with a red brick lamp room. Originally, Stanner was provided with one siding, mainly to accommodate traffic from the Gore quarry. In 1901, however, the Old

Radnor Lime, Roadstone & General Trading Co. applied for their own siding, the estimated cost of which (£247) would be refunded over a period of time by a 5% rebate on traffic. Apparently, this (second) siding was not built until 1914, by which time the cost had risen to £394, with an additional £12 for signalling.

A corrugated iron goods lock-up, approved in December 1897, was also provided at a cost of £46. A house for a station master was also approved in 1909, but

By 1951 the station was little used, and indeed was about to close to passengers.   *G. F. Bannister*

it is doubtful whether this was actually built. A hut was provided over the ground frame, which latterly had three levers, one for the facing point lock (released by a key on the staff) and two for working the switch blades.

Leaving Stanner, the line curved gently to the left, passing through flat countryside until after about one mile, it reached Dolyhir. This station served a straggle of hamlets such as Burlingjobb and Old Radnor as well as Dolyhir itself. The title, if spelt in the Welsh manner – *Dol-y-hir* – seems less curious, and its translation 'long meadow' more evident. Framed by two level crossings, each with a crossing keeper's house (and known quite prosaically as East and West crossings), the station was totally dominated by the lime works of the Old Radnor Trading Company. A slightly larger design of building was envisaged when the line was taking shape, and the need for a 'station at the lime works' first became apparent, but the reducing circumstances of the K & E dictated a smaller building, and a (possibly) more charming little structure was the result. Stanner was subsequently built to the same drawings, although in 'mirror image'.

A goods lock-up, again a small corrugated iron shed of standard GWR design, was also provided.

This '74XX' 0–6–0PT, shunting at the east end of Dolyhir station had just come to a stand beside the house at East Crossing, the gates of which were behind the photographer. The building on the left was a weighing machine office.   *R. H. Jobson*

In later years the paling fence seen above was removed, allowing this close-up view of the ground frame of levers for working the signals protecting the level crossing gates, and the gate interlocking.   *D. Clayton*

DOLYHIR STATION.

Dolyhir station c.1920. The gardens here were notable and included vases made at the works of the Old Radnor Trading Company. The ground frame at the far end of the platform covered the levers (released by a key on the train staff) working the siding points and facing point locks. This was in a different location from the 'signal box' shown on the plan, which was on the site occupied in this view by the hut with a sloping roof. The telegraph instrument was in the station office, as evidenced by the 'fault board' on the outside wall.

Collection Roger Carpenter

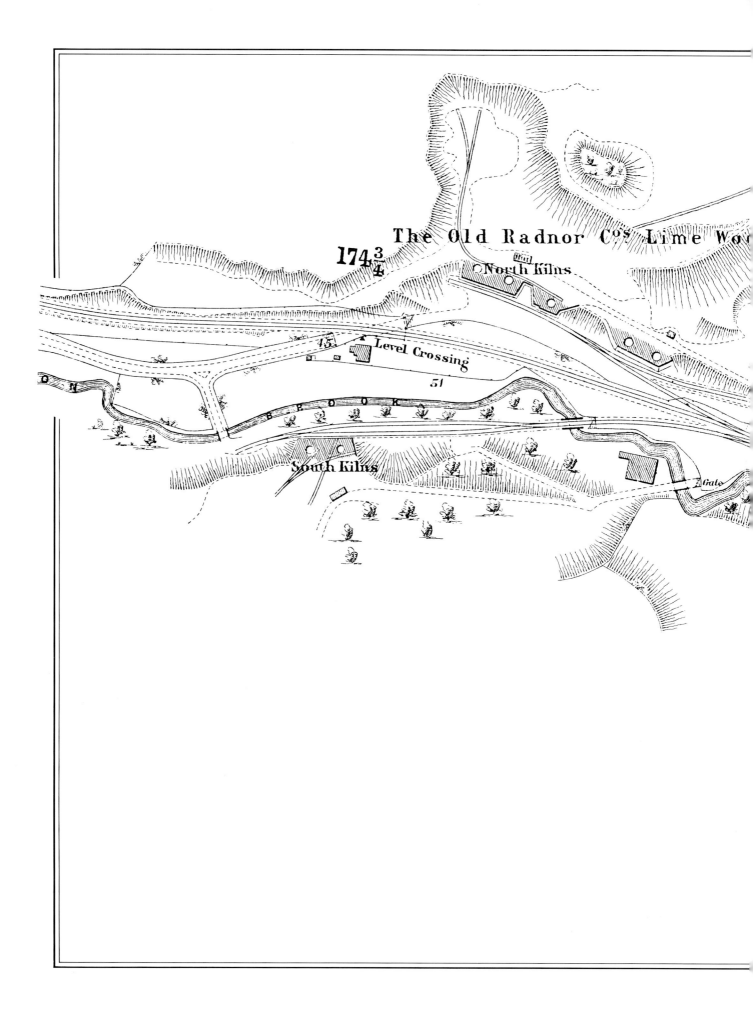

The Old Radnor C⁰ˢ Lime Wo

174.¾

North Kilns

Level Crossing

45

51

BROOK

ON

South Kilns

Gate

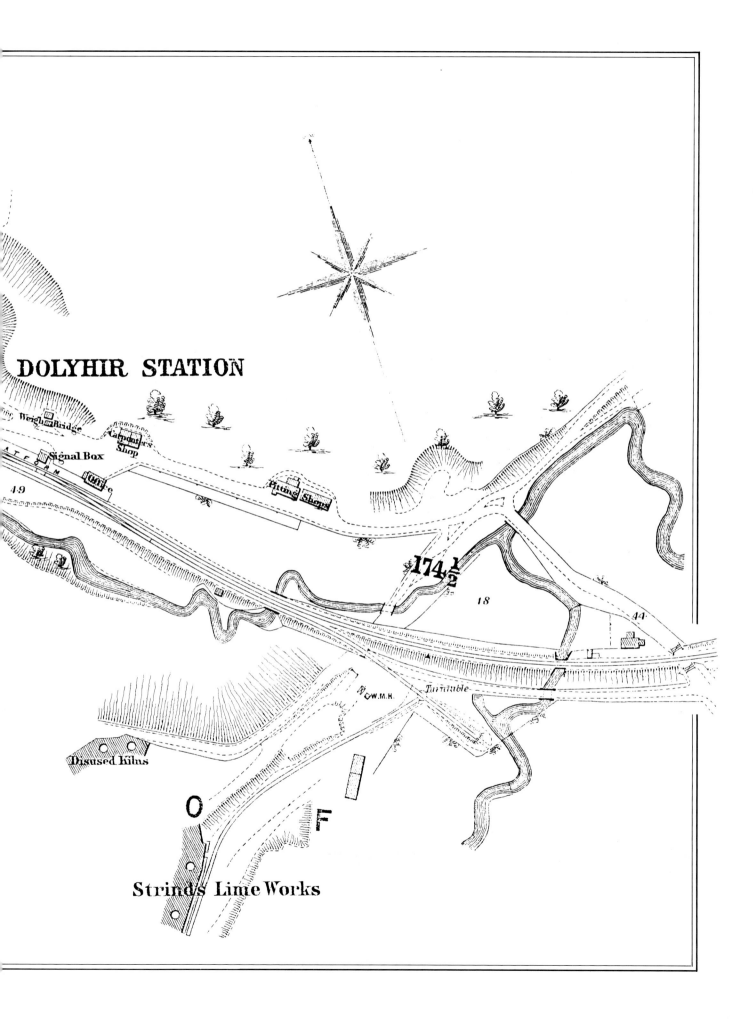

DOLYHIR STATION

Weigh Bridge

Carpenter's Shop

Signal Box

Office

PLATFORM

49

Fitting Shops

174½

18

44

G.W.M.H.

Turntable

Disused Kilns

O

F

Strinds Lime Works

Dolyhir station, originally the only intermediate station on the extension for which drawings were prepared. The design was subsequently used for the later station at Stanner and adapted for New Radnor. A public road ran behind the platform although it is hard to believe it in this sylvan view probably taken just after the First World War. The signal at the Kingston end of the platform was the up distant for East Crossing.   *L & GRP cty. David & Charles*

A similar view taken in June 1951.   *D. Clayton*

A view westwards from the end of the platform ramp at Dolyhir, towards New Radnor, in June 1951. The gated sidings led to the South Kilns (left) and the North Kilns (right). The distant signal warned down trains of the position of the gates of West Crossing, visible round the curve.

D. Clayton

This picture of Dolyhir in June 1951 shows how little the station changed over the years. The lorry is crossing the running line to gain access to the goods siding. The North Kilns of the Old Radnor Company's lime works can be seen in the background.   *D. Clayton*

Facing page: The up distant signal for West Crossing, Dolyhir, with the quarry behind North Kilns in the distance, in June 1951. The wheel in the finial carried the chain by which the signal lamp could be wound up and down (for filling, and to be extinguished during daylight hours to save oil) using the winch at the foot of the post (left-hand side). *D. Clayton*

After leaving the industrial environs of Dolyhir, the railway soon got back into real countryside and the New Radnor train is seen here midway between Dolyhir and Jerry's bridge with the hills about Gladestry in the background. The wooden occupation crossing gates were typical on the extension.

R. H. Jobson

R. H. Jobson

A rare glimpse of the Radnor Goods drifting downhill towards Kington in the vicinity of Jerry's Bridge.

Bryn Crossing was dominated by the brooding hills of Radnor Forest. This view, looking towards New Radnor, shows the 21ft rails of the 1890 relaying.
W. H. McKaig, cty. E. P. Jobson

In addition to domestic coal, there was a period just after the Second World War when fertiliser was also delivered by rail; barley and wheat had seemingly been grown on the ridge for some time.

The line left Dolyhir on a left-hand bend, and having straightened, crossed the minor road from Yardro to Harpton, which it then paralleled. Passing under Jerry's bridge, the third and last bridge over the line, the railway bore to the left, still in a cutting. Approaching Bryn crossing, Radnor Forest came into view, dominated by the distinctive dome of the Whimble (1,966ft), and finally a straight run along the bottom of The Smatcher (1,396ft) brought the line into New Radnor.

The station was as typical a terminus as one might expect in such a location, but the facilities, simple though they were, soon appeared generous in the light of the

Arrival at New Radnor.
J. D. Hewitt

Arrival at New Radnor. The loco is almost certainly No. 3574 and the photo was taken in 1947 at the latest as the loco was withdrawn soon after. The point disc in the right foreground was connected to the rod operating the switch blades and worked with them.

R. H. Jobson

From the same point, the entire station is spread out in this view taken in 1949. The route into the platform was not the straight one a legacy of the days when the station was planned as a possible passing loop on a line through to Rhayader.   *G. F. Bannister*

The four-lever ground frame at New Radnor was housed in a standard GWR hut (see the photo of Stanner on page 33) which seemed rather swamped by the cast iron nameboard. This photo was taken in June 1951.

D. Clayton

An atmospheric portrait of the branch train waiting to leave the terminus during the late 1940s.

L & GRP, courtesy David & Charles

sparse nature of the traffic. A small station building, goods shed, cattle dock and two sidings might have seemed to be a reasonable provision at the time of the opening, but even these limited facilities soon became superfluous. There was no loco shed, but with trains operating from Leominster, itself a busy junction with shed facilities, there was no necessity for one.

Cattle droving, the practice of bringing stock to market by shepherding it day after day from the hills over great distances, was already well into decline, and dwindled rapidly with the building of the railways. The New Radnor extension shortened the droving distance still further, and the cattle loading dock saw some use initially. However, the Central Wales line took an increasing proportion of the traffic, and the business dropped off sharply.

In 1903, certain alterations (estimated at £406) were carried out to the yard, including locking arrangements and the provision of a headshunt. This was a considerable sum, and it is believed that the improvements shown by the layout plans were carried out at that time. Curiously, the headshunt shown in the final plan of the station was not confirmed by the Ordnance Survey at any date.

New Radnor station was thereafter protected by a fixed distant signal and the only examples found at the

terminus were point discs protecting exit from the goods yard and a catch point at the east end of the loop. The lamp in/out repeater for the distant signal was located in the station office. A ground frame at the east end of the station, beyond the end of the loop, contained four levers, two of which were facing point locks released by a key on

Nature trying hard to reclaim her own in this view taken in 1949.
G. F. Bannister

No. 7437 was built in September 1948 and was being given a trial run over the branch when photographed at the terminus. The train of toplight coaches was not therefore typical of the stock normally used on the branch. *Rev. D. A. Tipper*

This 1950s view clearly shows the remote setting of New Radnor station and the beckoning hills which tempted those 19th century entrepreneurs and in the end thwarted them. The brick-built lamp hut is the most prominent building in this view, and looks in rather better condition than the cattle loading dock on the left.

Michael Hale

The rail-built loading gauge may possibly have replaced the wooden example on page 17 when the track alterations were undertaken. This photograph was taken in June 1951.

D. Clayton

This photograph, taken in 1952, gives a final look back at the approaches to the station and the beginnings of the afforestation which has so transformed the locality.

G. F. Bannister

The town of New Radnor viewed from the castle mound, just prior to the last war before the hills in the background became extensively afforested. The station was built some way from the edge of this small town and can be seen on the hillside beyond.   *R. H. Jobson*

the train staff. The point at the west end of the loop was worked by a lever positioned alongside.

The stone-built station building matched the others on the extension architecturally, except for a steeper roof pitch and different pattern of ornamental barge boards. Like the other stations, New Radnor did not boast a 'Ladies' toilet. Although there was a supply of water to the 'Gents', drinking water had to be brought from Kington in the time-honoured way, in old milk churns. The procedure for replenishing the water supply to the 'Gents' was to pump water from the tower in the yard

which in turn was refilled by further pumping from a local spring.

A public telephone was provided at the station, with an appropriate blue enamel sign situated on the platform elevation.

The goods yard was metalled in 1918; W.J. Crompton (Timber Merchant) contributed £25 to the cost, which was estimated at £80.

The most modern improvement noted was a new weighbridge in 1931, costing £340.

THE OLD RADNOR TRADING COMPANY

THE quarries that had justified the last few miles of the Kington Tramway produced limestone which, when burnt in a kiln, produced lime. This substance was used for agricultural purposes, being used to improve the land, and also as a flux in the steel-making process (for which purpose it was sent to South Wales). The manufacture of lime had been an expensive process, as coal had first to be taken to Dolyhir before the resultant material could be produced. Further, the operation had been on a relatively small scale when compared with later development.

As building of the railway progressed, the Chambers family (who were engaged in its construction) became aware of the quarries at Old Radnor, and investigated their potential. It was apparent that a form of roadstone, very similar to dhu stone from Clee Hill, was present on one side of the site, whilst the valuable limestone was to be found on the other.

Railway building was rapidly reaching saturation point, both from a geographical and financial viewpoint. The Chambers reasoned that the roads, hitherto largely neglected in a national sense, may well prove to be a good investment, especially with the continued development of steam-powered vehicles and such.

The arrival of the standard gauge railway, with all its connections, was clearly the key to the exploitation of

The Old Radnor Company had an aggressive marketing policy and established depots throughout the border counties of Radnor, Brecon, Hereford and Shropshire. This coal order office displays the company's new name following the change in 1901. Mr. Henry Stephens supplied a 'populous' area and an 'enlarged' office was opened there shortly after, surely not the subject of this particular photograph! Kingsland, c.1904.   *Courtesy Leominster Museum*

these potential reserves. The Old Radnor Trading Company was therefore formed in 1875, leasing the quarries from their owner, Sir Gilbert Lewis, Bart., a director of the Kington & Eardisley Railway. The chairman of the new company was Charles Chambers, whilst Mr. C. Wellington Lloyd was appointed manager; the latter's acumen was largely responsible for the subsequent success of the concern.

In 1890, the efficiency of quarrying operations was enhanced by the introduction of improved drilling, boring, blasting and crushing equipment, including a new steam-operated plant laid down on the south side of the valley. Similar steam plants were subsequently installed on the north side of the valley, and also at the so-called Gore macadam quarry, immediately to the north of Stanner station, where a siding was laid in to accommodate the growing traffic.

Apart from the normal products of the quarries, the company also developed 'granitic' stone, a form of concrete block suitable for quality building, for which they earned a gold medal. The material was capable of the highest enrichment, being used for porches and bal-

ustrades on several country houses in the area, as well as more mundane applications such as 'concrete cottages' close to the railway embankment between Lyonshall and Titley. Ornamental plant vases made of 'granitic' were to be seen on the platform of Dolyhir station. The rock was extracted following a monthly explosive charge – on one occasion bringing down 12,000 tons!

A significant amount of work was carried out for other railway companies, mostly in the form of paving slabs, platform copings, etc. The platforms of Newquay station were executed in 'granitic', as were those on the GWR's cut-off route to the West of England between Castle Cary and Langport, opened in 1905/6. Further afield, Old Radnor supplied fenceposts for railings in Norfolk. Ironically, the fenceposts on the New Radnor branch were made elsewhere!

The company's original name was 'The Old Radnor Lime, Roadstone, and General Trading Co. Ltd.' but, by a special resolution in 1901, it was changed to 'The Old Radnor Trading Co. Ltd.' Most photographs of the company's wagons seen so far date from c. 1910, and show that the words 'Trading' and 'Ltd' were omitted in the

The company's fleet of wagons numbered around 200 at its peak, which is thought to have been around the outbreak of the First World War, when this photograph was probably taken, showing a train of them in unfortunate circumstances. At least they appear to be empty so it would not have been too difficult to return them to the company's wagon repair shop at Dolyhir. Repairing their own wagons led to a noteworthy degree of consistency in lettering.
Author's collection

Another view of the accident, showing that wagon No. 159 had dumb buffers, along with several others of the same design. The location is the east end of Kington station, just yards from the signal box. *Collection Mike Lloyd*

These wagons were probably the earliest that the company owned and might have dated from the expansion in business following the installation of new quarrying equipment in 1890. Assuming this to be an official photograph on delivery, it is interesting to note the numerical sequence. It was quite a common practice to commence numbering a fleet of wagons at No. 100! The wagons display the full title of the company before it was shortened in 1901. *Collection Mike Lloyd*

An 1890s view of two of the North Kilns at Dolyhir reveals one of the elusive peak-roofed lime wagons.
Collection Mike Lloyd

A formal line-up of new steel-framed wagons outside two of the North Kilns c.1910.
Collection Mike Lloyd

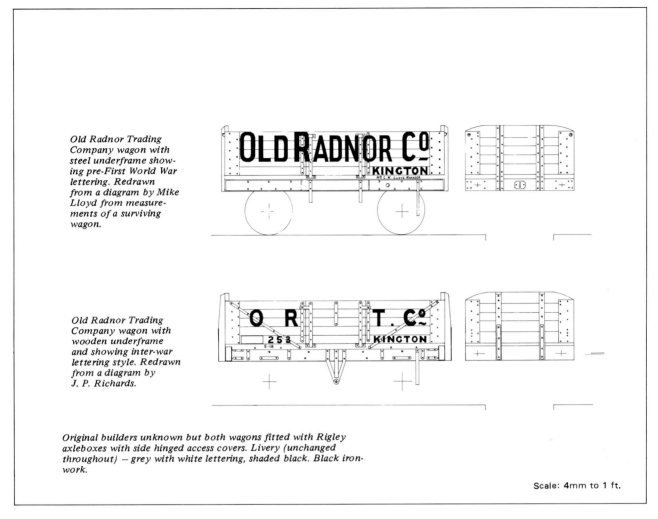

Old Radnor Trading Company wagon with steel underframe showing pre-First World War lettering. Redrawn from a diagram by Mike Lloyd from measurements of a surviving wagon.

Old Radnor Trading Company wagon with wooden underframe and showing inter-war lettering style. Redrawn from a diagram by J. P. Richards.

Original builders unknown but both wagons fitted with Rigley axleboxes with side hinged access covers. Livery (unchanged throughout) — grey with white lettering, shaded black. Black ironwork.

Scale: 4mm to 1 ft.

painted title; however, the earlier full title was known to be carried, unabridged. An even simpler livery was introduced in the 1920s. The wagon livery has been described as white lettering on a blue/grey body colour. The company also owned some peak-roofed lime wagons, the colour of which was believed to be red oxide, with white lettering.

The Old Radnor Co. owned about 200 wagons 'of the latest type' in 1906, about 50 of which were repainted and relettered each year. The company also owned a wagon repair shed, in which maintenance, repair and the repainting was carried out. It still owned 80 wagons when taken over by Mann Abel.

At an early stage of trading, the company became aware that its wagons would be returned empty to Dolyhir, and recognised that this situation was not economically ideal. So, the Old Radnor embarked on the business of coal merchandising, the success of which soon became apparent in its notably increased profits. As a member of the Coal Exchange, the company was able to purchase coal for cash, and send it direct from the colliery to their customers, carriage paid, to the required station. At colliery wholesale prices, they were thus able to defy competition both in quality and value. Their business was thus nationwide, and by establishing depots and agents at most stations in the counties of Hereford, Brecon, Radnor and Worcester, they acquired a virtual monopoly. Nevertheless, a number of independent coal merchants did manage to eke out a living in the area.

Nash Rocks owned a quarry (known as the 'Gore') which produced a superior roadstone. This was hauled to Stanner station by horse and cart for despatch in the firm's wagons, details of which are rather vague.

In 1905, the Old Radnor company built themselves new, prestigious offices in Kington, not surprisingly constructed in 'granitic' stone – the previous office had been partly demolished as an exercise by the local fire brigade! The new office building survives to this day as the town's public library.

NEW RADNOR STATION BUILDING

PUBLIC
TELEPHONE

NEW RADNOR LAMP HUT

Scale: 4mm to 1ft.

NEW RADNOR GOODS SHED

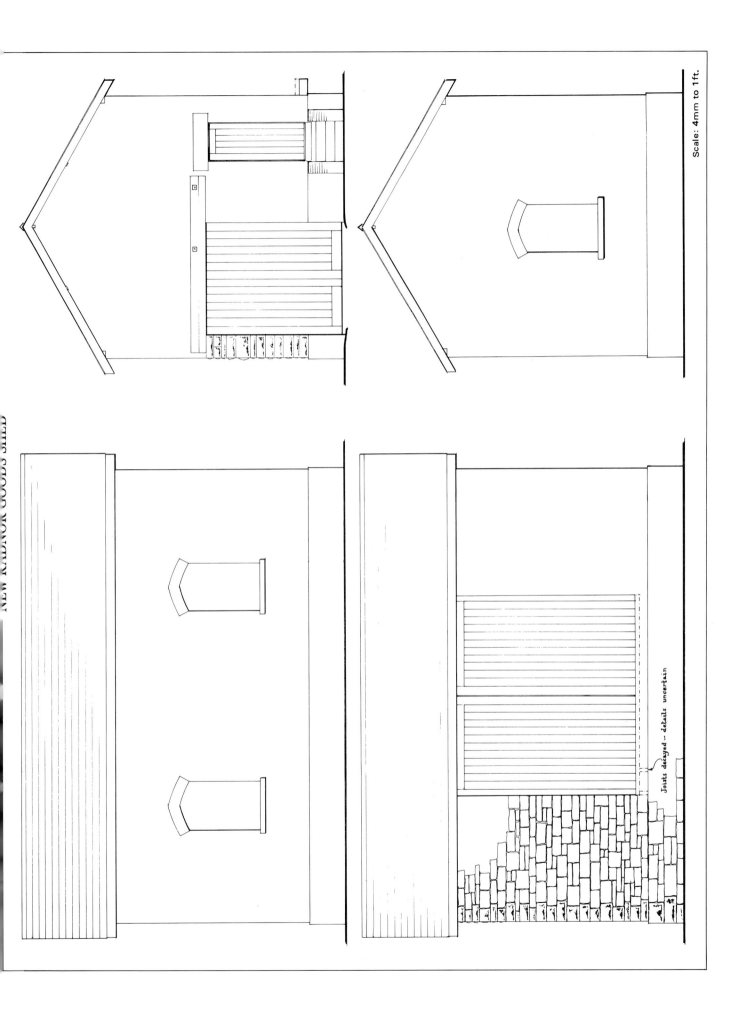

Joists decayed – details uncertain

Scale: 4mm to 1ft.

SINGLE LINE WORKING & SIGNALLING

The New Radnor extension was worked from its opening as a 'one engine in steam' line, using a wooden train staff (triangular in section on the centre part of its body, and painted green), fitted with a key to unlock points controlled by ground frames.

In the period 1902-1905 the signalling on the line was revised. At New Radnor the locking arrangements were altered, and a ground frame was all that was left to work the Kington end points, with a single fixed distant to act as a 'landmark'. For Dolyhir, a stud-locking frame for five levers was supplied in 1902, evidently to replace the 'signal box' arrangements which previously existed for working the points. At Kington the crossing loop was extended at the east end, and a scissors crossover installed between the new single line and the shunting neck (the former running line). A new signal box of 23 levers, including 3 spares, was provided as part of this work, which was inspected for the BoT on 21st June 1905.

For lightly used lines, the GWR made extensive use of the 'economic maintenance' system, under which gangers' lengths were substantially increased, and they were provided with mechanised trolleys for transport. Gangers' occupation keys authorised the occupation of the single line by the trolley, which could be removed from the line at a number of locations in mid-section. At each of these there was a box into which the key could be inserted, thus freeing the line for use by normal traffic.

The occupation key system was normally used on sections of line worked by electric train staff or electric key token, with which it could be electrically interlocked. It was hardly compatible with the working by a single wooden staff, nor was the introduction of ETS or EKT working likely to be justified on the New Radnor extension. A novel solution was produced.

The wooden staff for the section Kington–New Radnor was replaced by a 'Train Staff Key', which was much akin to a ganger's occupation key, except that it incorporated an Annett's key to allow the release of ground frame points. A very unusual four-slide control instrument was installed in Kington signal box.

The gangers' sections on the New Radnor extension were so arranged that one extended from 10 miles 60 chains past Kington signal box (13 miles 22½ chains) to 14 miles 70 chains. The second length was from 14 miles 70 chains to New Radnor (19 miles 65¾ chains). The 'Train Staff Key' section Kington–New Radnor thus fell into two gangers' sections. There was the further complication that the engine shed at Kington lay in the section, and the new apparatus allowed flexibility in working this siding as well.

The four slides of the control instrument were:

1. Control
2. Occupation Kington to 14 miles 70 chains
3. Occupation 14 miles 70 chains to New Radnor
4. Occupation Engine Sidings to Kington station only.

Each slide had three positions.

With all four slides fully in (position 1), the Train Key Instrument in Kington box could be used to obtain the key for the passage of a train. If one of the occupation keys was required, the Kington signalman pulled slide 1 to position 2. The man at New Radnor then pressed a plunger on his key instrument, and if the train staff key was locked up in an instrument at either Kington or New Radnor (so that there was no train in section, though there could be one at New Radnor station) the slide 1 could be pulled to position 3. This released mechanical locking within the control instrument so that any one of the other three slides could be withdrawn, or, if required, both 2 and 3 (gangers working on both lengths) could be drawn at the same time. When slide 4 was withdrawn, the Kington signalman could withdraw the 'to engine shed only' key from a separate instrument in his box.

CONTROL INSTRUMENT

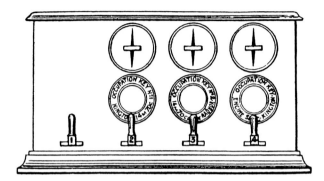

When the ganger had removed his trolley from the line, or the engine was on the engine shed siding and the siding points replaced to normal, the occupation key used could be placed in a lineside box. An electric release sent to Kington box then allowed all the slides to be replaced to position 1, and normal through working using the 'Train Staff Key' resumed.

Before the man at New Radnor went off duty each night, he had to give Kington a release to control slide 1, or the engine could not leave Kington shed next morning until the New Radnor man was on duty. The man at Kington had to remember not to put slide 1 to fully normal during this period, otherwise he lost the release!

All this equipment carried a maintenance cost, and the review of the line in 1925 estimated that £20 per year would be saved by reverting to a single wooden staff. A simple wooden staff, round and painted black, was noted in the record at Reading Signal Works on 30th April 1926 for the section 'Kington–New Radnor'. This staff had no key for the ground frame point on it, so apparently the train staff key was retained for a while as well. The works record for 14th December 1931 shows another staff for the Kington–New Radnor section, this time with a key fitted, again made round and painted black.

The extension ended its days worked by a simple wooden train staff.

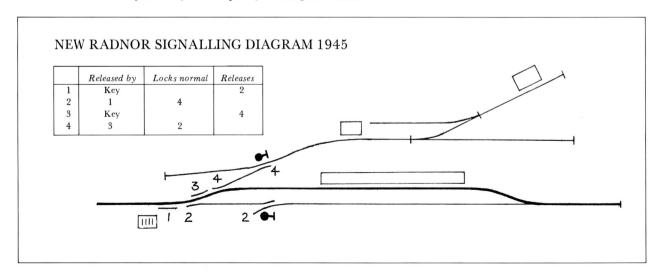

NEW RADNOR SIGNALLING DIAGRAM 1945

	Released by	Locks normal	Releases
1	Key		2
2	1	4	
3	Key		4
4	3	2	